ALL THE COLORS OF ME

AF898632

PICTURING MY WORRY

KNOWING AND SHOWING MY FEELINGS THROUGH ART

ANNA SHEPHERD
illustrated by ALICIA MÁS

PowerKiDS press

Published in 2027
by The Rosen Publishing Group, Inc.
2544 Clinton Street, Buffalo, NY 14224

First published in Great Britain in 2023 by Hodder & Stoughton
Copyright © Hodder & Stoughton Limited, 2023

Credits
Series Editor: Grace Glendinning
Series Designer: Alicia Más
Illustrations: Alicia Más

Every attempt has been made to clear copyright. Should there be any inadvertent omission please apply to the publisher for rectification.

The website addresses (URLs) included in this book were valid at the time of going to press. However, it is possible that contents or addresses may have changed since the publication of this book. No responsibility for any such changes can be accepted by either the author or the Publisher.

Cataloging-in-Publication Data
Names: Shepherd, Anna, author. | Más, Alicia, illustrator.
Title: Picturing my worry / Anna Shepherd, illustrated by Alicia Más.
Description: Buffalo, New York : PowerKids Press, 2027. | Series: All the colors of me
Identifiers: ISBN 9781499458886 (pbk.) | ISBN 9781499458893 (library bound) | ISBN 9781499458909 (ebook)
Subjects: LCSH: Worry in children--Juvenile literature. | Worry--Juvenile literature. | Emotions in children--Juvenile literature.
Classification: LCC BF723.W67 S547 2027 | DDC 155.41246--dc23

All rights reserved.
No part of this book may be reproduced in any form without permission in writing from the publisher, except by a reviewer.

Printed in China
CPSIA Compliance Information: Batch #QS27PK. For further information contact Rosen Publishing at 1-800-237-9932.

Find us on

CONTENTS

LISTENING TO WORRY

We all worry at times. Worry is a thought in our head that scares or upsets us a bit.

It might be about something **from the past ...**

... something that HASN'T HAPPENED YET ...

... or something that MAY NOT EXIST AT ALL, but feels very real!

It doesn't feel nice inside. We usually just want to make the worry go away, but **all feelings are really important.** They are trying to tell us something.

Worry is sending messages to help our brains learn and to keep us safe.

Learning to UNDERSTAND WORRY'S MESSAGES allows you to come up with ideas to HELP FIX IT.

There are lots of things we can do that can help us when we are having worries, big or small.

What are some things you do to help when you feel worried?

ART-MAKING CAN HELP

Doing art is a great way to understand what our worries are trying to tell us.

When we get worried, it can feel so big inside our head.

The pages of this book will help you see how **art can be a great tool to cope with worry.** For example …

PAINTING, DRAWING, DOODLING, or SCULPTING can HELP show and even CLEAR AWAY UNHELPFUL WORRIES.

When we look at what we have made, we might be surprised – maybe the worry **looks** much less scary than it **feels.**

Art is also **fun** and can make us feel **something new** entirely! By doing art we can **have a rest from worrying.**

You might think, "But I'm no good at art!" (Impossible!) But you don't have to worry about what it will look like. It is all about DOING. Then we see how the DOING helps us understand our feelings.

So let's get creative and see what happens!

We can begin by using art to get to know the idea of worry more clearly.

WORRY IS ...

usually a thought that stops you from enjoying yourself.

Worries can be tiny, right up to really huge!

No matter their size, worries come **from all sorts of places** and are **different** for everyone. Some worries even seem to come **from nowhere at all.**

Let's use your creative mind to get to know your worries.

First, draw or paint some of the things that you have worried about **in the past**. Make notes on the pictures to answer these questions:

Did this END UP being as BAD as you worried it would be?

If yes, what helped make it FEEL BETTER?

If you have worries **right now**, it can be helpful to draw them, too.

Some of them might be the same as in the past! Some might be new worries that you don't know very well yet.

Art can act like a magic mirror to help us see what our

WORRY LOOKS LIKE.

If you imagine "worry," what does it look like?

What COLOR is worry for you?
What SHAPE? Is it ALIVE?
MOVING or STILL?
What SOUND would it make?

Maybe it's like a big, **tangled** ball of wool.

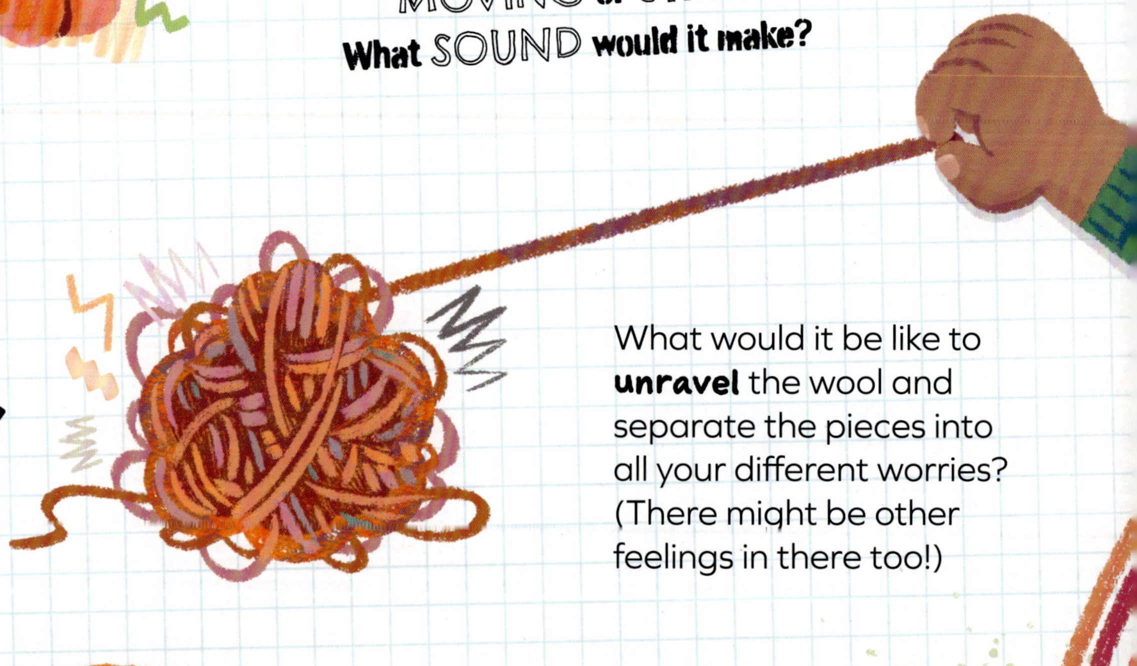

What would it be like to **unravel** the wool and separate the pieces into all your different worries? (There might be other feelings in there too!)

And what about how **we look** when we're worried?

Stand in front of a mirror and pretend to be worried. How do you hold your body? What are you doing with your shoulders? Your eyes? Put on your best worried face.

Draw a Worry Self-Portrait to help you think more about how you look when you're worried.

What kinds of **textures** and **colors** might fill your portrait? What kind of **marks** can you use to show the parts of you that feel the worry on the inside, where it doesn't show?

Now try being really cheerful in your body in front of the mirror. Does your body and face do anything different now?

Next we can use our portraits to start thinking more about what

WORRY FEELS LIKE.

our body gives us clues all the time about how we feel – we can be great feelings detectives!

Worry can feel **uncomfortable in our body.**

- WE MIGHT GET BUTTERFLIES IN OUR TUMMY.
- OUR HEADS MIGHT FEEL FILLED UP.
- OUR HEARTS CAN BEAT FASTER.
- OUR BODIES MIGHT FEEL TIGHT.
- WE CAN FEEL SICK, SAD, OR HEAVY INSIDE.

Use an imaginary magnifying glass and zoom in on different parts of your Worry Self-Portrait.

If you look at your tummy, how does worry feel there? Spiky or bumpy? Smooth or tight?

Could you PAINT that FEELING on or near your TUMMY in your portrait?

If you zoom in on your heart, can you listen closely to the thump-thump? Draw a frame around your picture, making a mark or zigzag with every thump.

How will your tummy TEXTURE and FRAME PATTERN CHANGE in your Cheerful Self-Portrait?

Next time you feel a worry coming along, remember how your body felt when you posed for your Cheerful Self-Portrait. Try changing how you stand and move, and see if it helps your worry to feel a bit different.

Just as we all **feel** worry differently, we all **show** it differently too. Do you know what your

WORRY ACTS LIKE?

When you spot a worry coming on, you may want to run away or hide.

Maybe it's hard to concentrate as your head feels too filled up with difficult ideas.

It can make it hard to play with friends and have fun.

We might cry, feel grumpy, or not want to talk.

Our voice might sound small and wobbly or big and booming.

Putting on a play with a trusted friend can be a great way to create art and get to know our worried behavior better.

Using your imagination, choose a worry that you have faced, which you and your friends can act out easily on stage.

Write the play, design the stage, and put on costumes to really set the scene!

Your performance could show:

1. how you behaved when facing this worry in real life
2. some ideas for how you did or could tell someone about your worry
3. some words of encouragement that would help you to feel better if you faced the worry again!

Now let's get even better at spotting the different

SHADES OF WORRY

that you may feel.

There are so many **words** that can describe **types of worry:**

Draw your own WORRY SCALE and faces to go with each worry word. Having this nearby can be really helpful to UNDERSTAND each new worry you face.

Experiment and play with paint to help you think even more about all these shades of worry! Mix different colors for each of the worry words.

What color would "anxious" be? Or "dread?" What happens if you add eco-glitter or mix in colors that make you feel happy, brave, or calm? How about adding water till the worry color fades?

Next time you have a **big worry,** use your Worry Scale to figure out how big it feels. Step away from the worry and do a **creative activity,** then come back to your scale and see if your worry level has changed! Why not try:

Dancing!

Fun and free movement gives your **mind a break** and helps you to **connect with your body.**

Get some trusted adults to do it too. Adults sometimes **forget** to **play** and their dancing might make you giggle!

Cooking!

Making and eating **healthy foods** is a very creative activity. It can clear your head and will **power your body and brain** to face big challenges. (Sugary food really doesn't help our moods.)

Singing!

What about singing really loudly to your **favorite song**?

Sometimes, our worry is so big that

SPEAKING OF WORRY

feels too big and tricky.

Occasionally people around you might find it hard to listen when you are worried. They want to take away your pain. They might tell you to just stop worrying or say:

But these words don't make the worry go away, do they?

No worry is silly; sometimes adults forget what being a child is like.

Art can help us show others what we really need when we're worried.

Imagine your **perfect listener**. What would you say to them about your worries if you could? **Draw a cartoon strip** of the scene.

And how would your PERFECT LISTENER reply?

You can share your unique comic with your trusted adults and friends so they can see how you would like to chat through your worries.

Can't find any words at all? Take out your Worry Scale and just point! Your loved ones will understand. Or just paint a picture of the worry if words and scales don't describe it quite right. Always remember it is OK to feel this way.

So, what do you do when you've tried lots of ideas, but you just

CAN'T STOP THE WORRY?

Sometimes worries **come and go**. We can shake them off without much trouble.

Other times, worries might stay around and we can't understand why. They **go round and round in our heads** and we can't think our way out of them.

What helps when you are feeling STUCK IN A WORRY?

Putting worries down on paper can help to show a way out.

They will look different on the paper instead of swirling about inside our head. We can step back from our worries and consider them.

And this is where art can give us a new view altogether.

Can you think of a BIG worry you've had recently? Paint it as a Giant Worry Beast, filling a full page with its hugeness.

Next, get a tiny piece of paper and paint the same beast really small. Does that change how you feel about it?

IMPORTANT! If our worry builds up until it feels like there is just too much to hold, we might need some extra help. Then, it is a good idea to talk to an adult you trust.

PRACTICING WORRY

means getting in the habit of knowing and sharing our worries.

Thinking and thinking about worry can make it get **bigger and BIGGER**. Then we find it harder to enjoy any happy moments, for example, when someone is being kind or funny, or when the sky looks beautiful.

So, if we practice feeding our minds more **helpful thoughts**, these will grow bigger instead, and might help the worries get a bit smaller.

Then we will also have more space in our heads to think about what to do with worries when they next appear.

Write out and decorate these helpful phrases and stick them somewhere so you don't forget them.

MY WORRY PLAN!

When I worry, I feel .... in my head and body.

When I am worried, I sometimes act

....

I can make my worries get smaller by

....

Why not fill your head with happy thoughts before you go to sleep! Make a scrapbook of things that make you happy – puppies, sunsets, ice cream, friends, family, video games – and browse through it before you go to sleep.

Find what works for you; we are all different, which is what makes us so interesting!

YOU ARE A WORRY ARTIST!

There are so many ways to be creative when you feel worried, and now that you've read this book, you are an expert feelings artist!

Here are even more fun ideas to keep your creativity flowing and your worries in balance.

How about making a Worry Chomper out of a box? Give it a big mouth. Write your worries on pieces of paper and post them into its mouth. Chomp up all those worries!

Make Worry Friends out of clothes pins. Before you go to sleep, tell them your worries and imagine them going off and sorting the worries out while you rest. What adventures will they have?

What about painting a worry every day for a week and seeing if it changes over time? (It probably will.)

Mon.	Tue.	Wed.	Thu.	Fri.	Sat.	Sun.

Or you can paint a picture of a stream and cut out some paper leaves. Write each worry on a leaf and place it on the water. Imagine them **floating downstream** and letting all the worries **go from your mind**.

Or try this in real life. Write on real leaves and drop them in a stream to float away.

CAREFUL! Ask an adult for help near the water.

Or you can draw pictures of birds and write the worries on their wings and imagine them **flying away** above the clouds.

If you can feel your worry getting bigger, give your mind something else to do. It can stop you getting into a panic.

Sense painting

Look around the room and find 5 things you can SEE. Sketch a quick "still life" of these things on your paper.

Find 4 things you can TOUCH. Where will these fit into your picture?

Notice 3 things you can HEAR. How can you show these sounds filling the page?

What about 2 things you can SMELL? Notice them as you work on your art.

And imagine 1 thing you can TASTE. (Just in your mind!) Can you add yourself to the painting, taking a happy bite of it?

Let's try some free-form art using big blobs of paint and different tools (with permission!).

Explore your worries through new textures, using forks or a rolling pin to spread the paint, or some string or a sponge dragged through it. Have fun – experiment!

THEN, IF YOU FEEL COMFORTABLE: CRUMPLE UP, RIP UP, OR CUT UP THE PAPER FULL OF WORRIES, LETTING THEM GO.

When you think about past worries that didn't happen, make art to remind your brain that lots of your worries don't actually come true (or don't turn out quite as badly as you feared).

Congratulate yourself that you have managed so far!

Design and make yourself a WORRY TROPHY for looking after your feelings so well.

Can you think of other ways to make fun art? I think you have a BIG imagination ready for many different shades of worry.

KEY TERMS

Anxious: showing or feeling a worry about something, usually with an outcome you're not sure about.

Balance: when emotions are steady, even, and stable.

Creativity: using your imagination to create something.

Encouragement: words or actions that make someone else feel brave or proud.

Pattern: a design or detail that is repeated.

Portrait: an image of a person.

Scrapbook: a book filled with memories, words, and images that relate to an experience or person.

Shades: slightly different varieties of something, such as a color.

Still life: a piece of art that shows things that do not move.

Texture: the feel or look of the surface of something.

Unravel: to unwind or pull apart something, for example, something made of yarn or string.

BOOKS TO READ

***Kids Can Cope* series,**
by Gill Hasson (Franklin Watts)

- *Bounce Back from Disappointment*
- *Face Your Fears*
- *Let Go of Jealousy*
- *Put Your Worries Away*
- *Say Hi When You're Shy*
- *Step Back from Frustration*
- *Take Charge of Anger*
- *Turn Away from Teasing*

***A World Full of Feelings* series,**
by Louise Spilsbury (Franklin Watts)

- *Finding Calm*
- *Finding Courage*
- *Finding Happiness*
- *Finding Kindness*

***Build Resilience* series,**
by Honor Head (Franklin Watts)

- *Anxiety and Self-esteem*
- *Coping with Change*
- *Friendships and Bullying*
- *Unexpected Challenges*

WEBSITES to **VISIT** with the help of an adult:

Headspace.com

A website and app offering meditation and mindfulness tools to expand on the practice of understanding and dealing with emotions.

Youthmindfulness.org

Resources for mindfulness programs for young people.

HOW TO USE THIS BOOK: A GUIDE FOR ADULTS

This series of art therapy books has been developed to provide a creative starting point for further discussion and exploration around children's emotions.

Each book is intended for children to **share** with trusted adults, whether one-on-one or in a group setting in the classroom or elsewhere.

This book, *Picturing My Worry*, is a careful exploration of the look and feel of all kinds of worries. When dealing with any tricky emotion, big or small, the utmost priority is making children feel **safe and heard** as they think things through.

Whether sharing at home or in a group setting, plan to begin at a time when you and your child or group are relaxed and have an uninterrupted moment to share an activity. It is important that the adult leading the activity is emotionally available when sitting to do this. This can be hard when you feel rushed and stressed, so choose the timing carefully.

Only you will know how much time and energy you and your child or group are able to give to this practice in each session, and what will suit your setting – dip in; read it completely; return to it again at times in the future. No matter what, **don't push things** – try out the bits that your child or group are most drawn to. Have a go at different activities when they feel right for the progression of the individual or group. Use each approach at a time and place that is **most helpful**.

The activities are catalysts for conversations about how children feel. Once the creativity starts flowing, the session may well grow beyond what's in these pages. Maybe a child has their own ideas about ways to feel a bit better that they could share with you or the group? Try to **listen** and not offer unwelcome solutions or critiques. It can be hard when you want to help, but trust that **with love, support, and encouragement,** children can usually find their own way through.

Also, take **notice of your own feelings** and responses as your child or group creates, and be mindful that you are modelling how to manage and regulate emotions. You do not need to get it right all the time; **be kind to yourself**, just as we encourage the children to be throughout this book. Helping children is not always easy.

In a group setting it is very important to make sure every child feels safe to share and participate. Establish a rapport of **support** and **zero judgement** of their art and expression of emotion.

But keep in mind that some children may need to have additional, dedicated help beyond what is appropriate to do on your own in a classroom or group setting. See page 32 for quick-reference contacts if you feel your child or group member needs further professional or anonymous assistance.

If you are concerned that a child is struggling to cope, then it is worth seeking advice from a professional.

American Art Therapy Association
arttherapy.org/art-therapist-locator

Learn more about art therapy and find a trained therapist to continue emotional work with a creative approach.

Find a Warmline
www.warmline.org

Warmlines are confidential, free phone services that offer emotional support to people who just need someone to talk to. Find a Warmline near you here.

Kids Help Phone
1-800-668-6868
kidshelpphone.ca

Kids Help Phone is a Canadian e-mental health service for youths with counselors available 24 hours a day.

National Mental Health Hotline
1-866-903-3787
mentalhealthhotline.org

This free, 24-hour help line connects people in need with caring, knowledgeable, licensed mental health counselors.

Nemours Kids Health
kidshealth.org

This website is full of helpful health resources for parents, kids, teens, and educators.